Music, Music, Music!

Contents

The Magic of Music	4
Musical Styles	
Classical Sounds	6
Pop Goes Bang!	8
Folk from the Heart	10
Musical Families	12
Stringing Us Along	14
Bold As Brass	16
The Rhythm of the Beat	18
Stomp!	20
Tinkling the Ivories	22
Plugging In	24
The Language of Music	26
Sing Out Loud	28
Glossary	30
Index and Bibliography	31
Research Starters	32

Features

Turn to **Stomp!** on page 20 to read about a percussion group who use wooden poles, brooms, garbage cans, and hubcaps to make music!

Do you know which instrument has a name that means "soft-loud"? Find out in **Do You Play the Soft-Loud?** on page 22.

Who wrote some of the world's greatest classical music despite going deaf? Discover the answer on page 23 and learn more about this incredible musician.

Eleven-year-old Olivia Stephenson is singing her way to success. Check it out in **Sing Out Loud** on page 28.

How can sound be seen?
Visit www.rigbyinfoquest.com
for more about MUSIC.

The Magic of Music

Beats, rhythms, songs, and tunes, call them what you will, they are all music. Many people enjoy creating and making music. Many more enjoy listening to the music of others. Musical appreciation reaches across boundaries of culture and time. Like all art forms, music can be used to express feelings and ideas. In a way, music is an international language. People from different countries, with very different lifestyles, often understand and enjoy the same kinds of music.

Music serves many purposes. It is a fundamental part of many cultural, religious, and social ceremonies. It is also an essential component of dance and theater around the world. Last but not least, music can make people feel happy and relaxed.

Can you imagine what it would sound like if the animals, the plants, the wind, the sky, and Earth had a conversation? This is how some people describe the music produced by a didgeridoo—a sacred Aboriginal wind instrument from Australia.

Above: Belonging to a school **orchestra** or **band** is popular around the world. This school orchestra is in Malaysia.

Left: This musician in Korea is playing a stringed instrument called a koto.

Musical Styles

There are many different musical styles around the world. Western music, the major form of music played and heard in the Americas, Europe, Britain, Australia, and New Zealand, can be divided into three main types: classical music, popular music, and folk music.

Classical Sounds

Classical music is **composed** according to rules and is written down. It includes very long pieces of music called **symphonies** and music for operas and ballets.

An orchestra is led by a conductor who stands in front of the musicians. The conductor waves a baton or uses his or her hands to indicate to the musicians how fast or slow a piece of music should be, and how loud or soft each part should be played.

PROFILE

Wolfgang Amadeus Mozart (1756–1791)

All of the great classical composers were musical geniuses, but only a few created masterpieces as children. At the age of three, Mozart taught himself to play a keyboard instrument called the harpsichord by listening to his older sister practice. At four, he was writing his own music, and at five, he gave his first public performance. His father, who was also a musician, realized that the young Wolfgang had incredible talent and made sure that he learned from the best teachers in Europe. Mozart went on to write his first symphony at the age of eight and his first opera at the age of eleven. Mozart's life was not long, but he used it well, producing over 600 musical works which included long operas and symphonies.

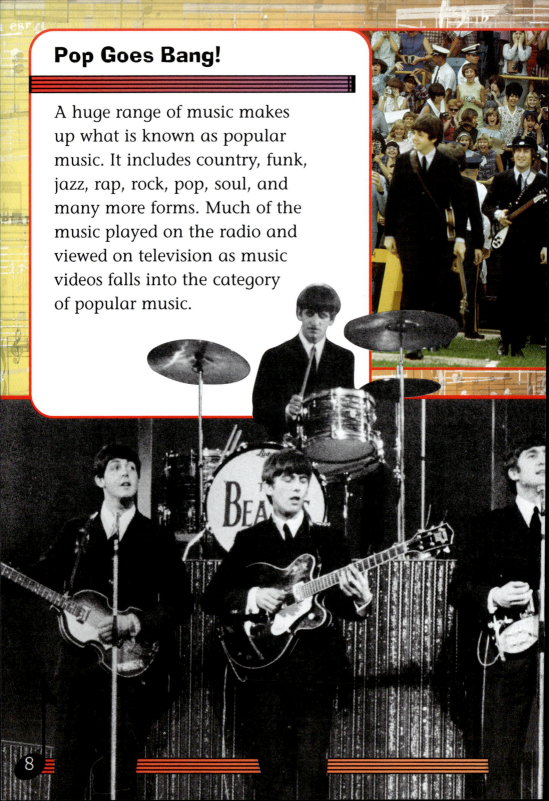

Pop Goes Bang!

A huge range of music makes up what is known as popular music. It includes country, funk, jazz, rap, rock, pop, soul, and many more forms. Much of the music played on the radio and viewed on television as music videos falls into the category of popular music.

Musical Styles continued

In the early 1960s, a band burst onto the international music scene and changed the direction and future of popular music forever. This band from Liverpool, England, was called The Beatles. In their early years, The Beatles' style was influenced by American rock artists such as Chuck Berry, Buddy Holly, and the Everly Brothers. The Beatles developed pop music further, however, by increasing the emphasis on **melody** and **lyrics.** Everywhere they performed, The Beatles created a sensation. Huge numbers of young fans watched their every move, following fashions they set in clothing and hairstyles. The phenomenon of Beatlemania was born as the importance and influence of music that appealed to young people exploded across the Western world.

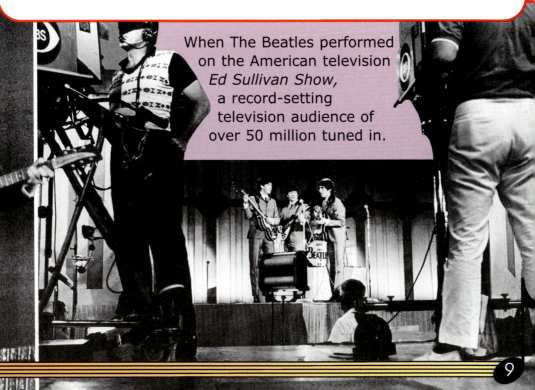

When The Beatles performed on the American television *Ed Sullivan Show*, a record-setting television audience of over 50 million tuned in.

Folk from the Heart

Folk music largely consists of traditional songs that have developed over a long period of time within communities. Some folk songs have been passed on from generation to generation for hundreds of years.

Today, the term "folk music" is also often used to describe songs that tell stories about ordinary, everyday people. One of the most influential American folk musicians of the twentieth century was Woody Guthrie. His songs spoke for everyone, especially the poor. Woody Guthrie wrote **ballads** about the hard luck and courage of migrants during the **Depression.** He wrote songs for factory workers who were trying to get better working conditions and higher pay. Perhaps the greatest of Guthrie's achievements, however, was that he inspired future generations of folk musicians.

Canadian musician Joni Mitchell is well-known for her rich folk lyrics and strong voice.

Musical Styles continued

Joan Baez (born 1941)

Banjo

Growing up in the 1960s as English-Scottish and Mexican American, Joan Baez learned about racial discrimination the hard way. This was one of the experiences that led her to become a great folk musician. Many of Baez's ballads are protest songs. From the 1960s on, she has used her music to protest against war and racism, promoting peace and human rights.

When Woody Guthrie died in 1967, he had written more than 1,000 songs, including the American classic "This Land Is Your Land."

Woody Guthrie

Musical Families

There are hundreds of different kinds of instruments, and they all produce their own sounds. Most musical instruments have a string, a **reed**, or some other device that creates sound waves when it moves. Despite the differences in the way instruments may look, they can all be placed into five major classes: (1) strings, (2) wind, (3) percussion, (4) keyboard, and (5) electronic.

Instruments from many different countries and played by many different cultures all fit into these five categories.

The guitar, a stringed instrument, is common in many forms of music. This musician is playing Mexican music known as *mariachi*.

How can sound be seen?
Visit www.rigbyinfoquest.com
for more about MUSIC.

Stringed Instruments

There are two basic types of stringed instruments: those that are bowed, such as the violin, and those that are plucked, such as the harp. Stringed instruments also include the banjo, bass, cello, guitar, harp, lute, lyre, mandolin, sitar, violin, and zither.

Wind Instruments

Wind instruments include woodwind instruments, such as flutes and pipes, and brass instruments, such as trumpets. Both are played by blowing into or through a tube. Wind instruments include the bugle, clarinet, flute, horn, oboe, pipes, recorder, saxophone, and tuba.

Percussion Instruments

Percussion instruments make music either by being shaken or hit. The most common percussion instruments are drums, but the glockenspiel, xylophone, triangle, gong, castanet, tambourine, and marimba also fall into this category.

Keyboard Instruments

All keyboard instruments have keys that a musician must press to produce sound. Some keyboards control hammers that strike strings. Others activate a device to pluck strings or push air through pipes. The piano, harpsichord, and pipe organ are all keyboard instruments.

Electronic Instruments

Instruments that produce electronically amplified sound, such as the electric guitar, can produce a wider variety of sounds than the same non-electric instruments.

Stringing Us Along

When the player of a stringed instrument makes one or more strings vibrate, it produces sound. The violin family is made up of four instruments: the violin, the viola, the cello, and the double bass. As the instruments get bigger, their **pitch** gets lower. Violins and violas are played positioned under the chin. The cello is played sitting down, and the double bass is played standing up. All of these instruments are played with a bow, although they can also be plucked. This method of playing a double bass is very common in jazz music.

Plucked stringed instruments are played by plucking the strings, either with the fingers or a small object called a pick. The most common plucked instrument is the guitar.

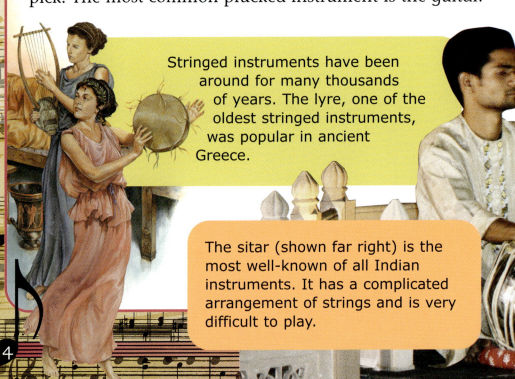

Stringed instruments have been around for many thousands of years. The lyre, one of the oldest stringed instruments, was popular in ancient Greece.

The sitar (shown far right) is the most well-known of all Indian instruments. It has a complicated arrangement of strings and is very difficult to play.

Bold As Brass

When we think of wind instruments, we may think of the booming sounds of a brass band. Some woodwind instruments such as the flute, however, can produce music that is soft and delicate. Like all flutes, the panpipe is played by blowing air across the top of a pipe. This makes the air inside the pipe vibrate and produces a musical note. A long pipe holds more air and produces a lower note than a short pipe.

Have you ever heard the haunting, shrill tones of a bagpipe? The bagpipe is an unusual wind instrument that consists of a leather bag with five wooden pipes. The player blows air through a blowpipe and presses the holes in one of the pipes, called the chanter, to produce music. The bagpipes are a traditional instrument of Scotland.

Panpipe

Musical Families continued

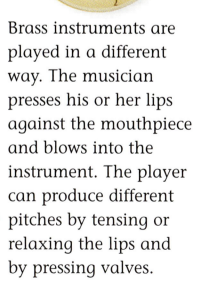

Tuba

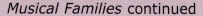

PROFILE

Charlie Parker (1920–1955)

Charlie Parker was a famous jazz musician and composer. He played the alto saxophone, a woodwind instrument that has a reed attached to the mouthpiece.

In the early 1940s, Charlie Parker, along with some other musicians, began experimenting with a new, complicated form of jazz which came to be known as bebop. This new style was only for musicians with excellent technique.

In the years that have followed, many saxophonists have copied Parker's style of playing long solos with many different notes, difficult timing, and unusual melodies.

Brass instruments are played in a different way. The musician presses his or her lips against the mouthpiece and blows into the instrument. The player can produce different pitches by tensing or relaxing the lips and by pressing valves.

The Rhythm of the Beat

Percussion instruments vary hugely in appearance and the sounds they produce. Their volume is controlled by the amount of force used to hit them, shake them, or scrape them. The rhythmic sound of a beating drum is an important part of many cultural rituals and celebrations. When the head of a drum is hit, it vibrates, causing the air inside the drum to ring with sound. A smaller or tighter head produces a higher note than a larger or looser head.

Many percussion instruments produce a sound rather than a musical note. These instruments are called unpitched percussion. The way to figure out if a percussion instrument is pitched or unpitched is to see if you can sing the note it makes. If you can, it is a pitched instrument but if you cannot, it is unpitched.

Steel drum

The steel drum is from Trinidad in the West Indies. As its name suggests, each instrument is made from a steel oil drum. Steel drums are an important part of local carnival celebrations.

Musical Families continued

Members of the Shasta Taiko drumming group (shown below) perform both traditional and contemporary pieces using age-old Japanese drums and techniques.

Vibraphone

Sleigh bells

Stomp!

Take a range of everyday household items, add a pair of creative thinkers, and mix together eight talented performers. What do you get? The answer is *Stomp*—a vibrant, energy-filled musical performance. The sound is percussive, but there is not a traditional percussion instrument in sight. Explosive rhythms are produced using objects as diverse as brooms, paint scrapers, and garbage cans. The effect is unique, and audiences have flocked to see what the *Stomp* noise is all about.

Musical Families continued

Stomp was created in England in 1991 by Luke Cresswell, Steve McNicholas, and a group of street performers. After winning awards in Britain, they took *Stomp* around the world, picking up more awards nearly everywhere they performed. One of the great things about *Stomp* on tour is that the organizers invite local talent to join in the show. This means that both audiences and musicians worldwide are getting the opportunity to explore the unique sounds of *Stomp*.

Tinkling the Ivories

The piano is a common instrument in Western music, and it is a popular choice for people who want to learn to play music. A piano has sets of wire strings that are stretched tightly over an iron frame. Each set of strings has a hammer. When the player strikes the keys, either gently or strongly, the hammer strikes the strings with the same force and makes them vibrate. The long strings make low notes and the short strings make high notes.

The keyboard of a piano has 52 white keys and 36 black keys.

Foot pedals are used to change the length and volume of a note.

Do You Play the Soft-Loud?

Until the early 1700s, keyboard instruments could only produce soft sounds. Then, in 1709, an Italian instrument maker named Bartolomeo Cristofori created a keyboard instrument that used hammers to strike strings. This produced both soft and loud sounds, or in Italian, *piano* and *forte* sounds. The *pianoforte*, as it was soon called, developed into today's piano.

Musical Families continued

Grand piano

Ludwig van Beethoven (1770–1827)

Beethoven was one of the greatest pianists and composers who ever lived. His achievements were astounding, even more so when you realize that for many years Beethoven wrote music that he couldn't hear!

At the age of 30, Beethoven began to go deaf. He broke the strings of his piano by pounding on the keys in an effort to hear his music. Eventually, deafness forced him to stop playing, however, he continued to write music until he died. His last symphony was written when he was completely deaf!

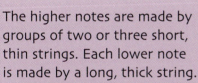

The higher notes are made by groups of two or three short, thin strings. Each lower note is made by a long, thick string.

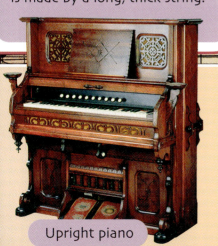

Upright piano

Plugging In

Plugging in instruments to increase and change their sound was the most exciting musical development of the twentieth century. Unlike their **acoustic** counterparts, most electric guitars and violins do not have hollow bodies. The bodies are usually made from solid wood. When an electric instrument is not plugged into an amplifier, it makes only a very small sound. When it is plugged in, two or more devices known as pickups convert the vibrations of the strings into an electrical signal.

The electric microphone was invented in 1916. It works by converting sound waves into electrical signals. An amplifier strengthens these signals, which are then passed to a loudspeaker. The loudspeaker changes the signals back into amplified sound waves that we hear as increased volume.

Musical Families continued

Much of the modern music we buy or hear on the radio has been created, at least in part, using synthesizers, samplers, and computers. Synthesizers can produce many sounds, including imitations of other instruments and entirely new noises.

A drum machine is a synthesizer that makes drum sounds and rhythms. Since the early 1980s, drum machines have replaced real drummers on many recordings. Although they often sound nothing like real drums, their deep bass sounds and rock-steady timing make them ideal for dance music.

A more recent type of electronic drum is one that looks like a normal drum kit and is played by a live drummer. However, the "drums" are actually buttons which play a range of electronic sounds when struck.

Drum machine

Vanessa-Mae Vanakorn Nicholson is a star of the electric violin. She plays everything from classical to pop.

The Language of Music

When we listen to music, it is difficult to imagine a way in which it could be written on paper. However, music does have its own form of written language. This language, called notation, was first begun by monks in the 800s. Before then, all music was learned by heart or it was forgotten as soon as it had been played.

A written piece of music is called a score. Scores can be written for one instrument or for many. When a score is written for an orchestra, for example, the notes for different instruments are written above one another. It is important that composers write their music so musicians know what notes to play, the speed to play them, and even the mood the composer wants the music to achieve.

This score for a stringed instrument called a zither was created in the 1400s. It looks quite different from modern scores.

Musical notes are written on a set of five lines or in the four spaces between the lines. These lines are called a staff, or stave. Each line and space is used for a different note. A saying and a word can help you remember the notes.

Every **G**ood **B**oy **D**oes **F**ine

F A C E

Composing music on a computer is becoming very popular because you can immediately hear what you have composed played back through the computer's speakers.

MY DIARY

Sing Out Loud

THIS IS ME

I've been singing since I was three. I guess you could say that music is one of the most important things in my life. Mom suggested that I put together a scrapbook about my singing. So here it is!

Practice, Practice, Practice, Practice

Going to auditions is one of the most exciting things that I do. Before an audition, I often have butterflies. But when it's all over, I feel great—especially if I get the part!

I GOT THE PART!

I've been writing my own songs for as long as I can remember. I have a folder full of them. When I grow up, my dream is to write and sing my own songs—to be a pop star! I know this will be hard, but when it comes to singing, I've never given up yet!

This photo of me and two of my friends was in our local newspaper. It was taken after I had recorded the theme song for a campaign about energy. It was pretty cool because the song, with posters and an activity pack, was designed to teach kids about saving energy. I guess I got to be a bit of a star, while promoting a good cause!

Olivia
That's me!

MY WEEK

Monday
violin lessons

Tuesday
singing lessons

Wednesday
day off

Thursday
piano lessons

Friday
audition day

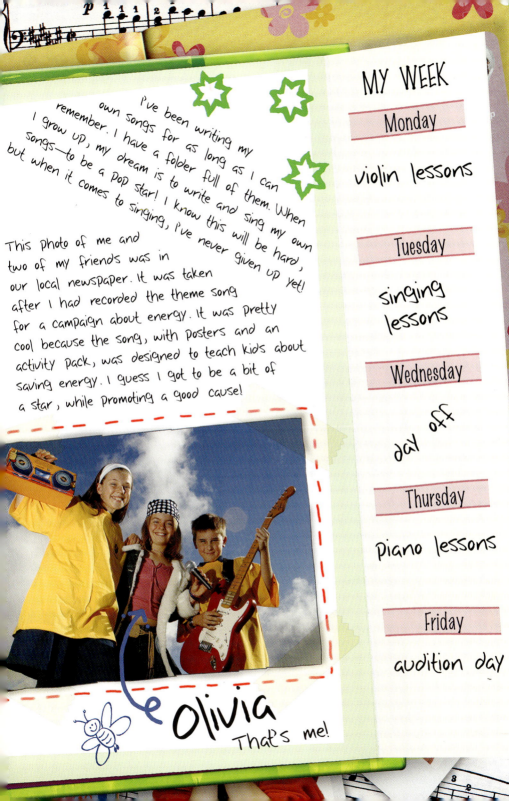

Glossary

acoustic – a musical instrument that is not electronically amplified

ballad – a song or poem that tells a story in short verses

band – a group of musicians who play together, largely on wind and percussion instruments

compose – to write or create music. A person who composes music is called a composer.

Depression – a period of time that started in 1929 and lasted throughout the 1930s. During the Depression, many banks and businesses closed and thousands of people lost their jobs. The Depression began in the United States and spread throughout the world.

lyrics – the words of a song

melody – the main tune in a musical piece

orchestra – a group of musicians who play together on various instruments. Some African and Asian orchestras are made up entirely of percussion instruments. In most Western countries, a musical group is considered to be an orchestra only if it contains violins and other stringed instruments.

pitch – a musical tone's degree of highness or lowness

reed – a piece of thin cane or metal in the mouthpiece of an instrument. A reed vibrates to produce sound.

symphony – a long, complex piece of music that is played by a full orchestra. A symphony is usually divided into four movements, or sections.

Index

composers and musicians
- Baez, Joan — 11
- Beatles, The — 8–9
- Beethoven, Ludwig van — 23
- Guthrie, Woody — 10–11
- Mitchell, Joni — 10
- Mozart, Wolfgang Amadeus — 7
- Parker, Charlie — 17
- Vanakorn Nicholson, Vanessa-Mae — 25

instruments
- electronic — 12–13, 24–25
- keyboard — 7, 12–13, 22–23
- percussion — 12–13, 18–21, 25
- strings — 5, 12–15, 24–25
- wind — 4, 12–13, 16–17

Bibliography

- Ardley, Neil. *Music.* Dorling Kindersley, 1989.

- Guthrie, Woody and Pete Seeger. *This Land Is Your Land.* Little, Brown & Company (Canada) Ltd., 1988.

- Jessop, Joanne. *Famous Musicians.* Wayland (Publishers) Ltd., 1993.

Research Starters

1 There are many musical instruments that are simple to make. Research to find instructions on how to make an instrument of your choice, or design your own instrument and write construction directions for a friend to follow.

2 Choose your favorite musicians and research about their lives and their musical influences. What music did they enjoy when they were young? What music do they listen to now? How did they become successful musicians?

3 Styles of popular music change over time. Interview older members of your family to find out what kind of music they enjoyed as teenagers. Do they still enjoy this music?

4 Choose a country other than your own and research to learn more about the instruments, techniques, and musical styles of that place. How do they compare and contrast with music that is familiar to you?